A KID'S GUIDE TO FEELINGS

FEELING HAPPY

BY KIRSTY HOLMES

Written by:
Kirsty Holmes

Edited by:
Holly Duhig

Designed by:
Danielle Rippengill

Image Credits

All images are courtesy of Shutterstock.com, unless otherwise specified. With thanks to Getty Images, Thinkstock Photo and iStockphoto. Front Cover – MarinaMay, yayasya, jirawat phueksriphan, Piotr Urakau, Samuel Borges Photography, Rawpixel.com, Kobsoft, Sergiy Bykhunenko. Images used on every page – MarinaMay, yayasya, Piotr Urakau. 2 – Strix, Sudowoodo. 5 – Frame Studio, Andrii Symonenko, Sudowoodo. 6 – Makc, Andrii Symonenko, Sudowood. 7 – Strix. 8 – Rawpixel.com, Maryna Kulchytska, TinnaPong. 9 – Daxiao Productions, VaLiza, travelview, Rawpixel.com. 11 – Mark Nazh, Africa Studio, naluwan. 12 – Samuel Borges Photography, ViChizh. 12 & 13 – Evellean. 13 – ColorBolt. 14 – gst, Khomenko Serhii, Strix. 15 – espies, Billion Photos, 3445128471. 16 – aliaksei kruhlenia. 17 – Luis Louro. 18 – KK Tan. 19 – Strix. 21 – Elena Nichizhenova, Rawpixel.com, 5 second Studio, VaLiza. 22 & 23 – Sudowoodo, Andrii Symonenko.

CONTENTS

Words that look like **this** can be found in the glossary on page 24.

INTRODUCING....

| CAN'T-WAIT-A GATOR | THE LONE FURBALL | SHRINKING VIOLET | RAGING RACCOON | CAPTAIN CHEERFUL | DR GLOOM | GREEN-EYED BUNNY | AGENT AFRAID |

AGENTS OF F.E.E.L.S!

FEELING.EVERY.EMOTION.LIKE.SUPERHEROES!

We all have **emotions**, or feelings, all the time. Our feelings are very important. They help us think about the world around us, and know how we want to **react**.

Sometimes, we feel good. Other times, we feel bad.

Captain Cheerful loves to play with Cocoa the cat.
Captain Cheerful is feeling really happy.

Let's find out more…

HOW DO WE FEEL WHEN WE'RE HAPPY?

You might feel really **relaxed**…

…you might feel warm all over…

…or you might feel like your chest or belly is really full.

HOW DO WE LOOK WHEN WE'RE HAPPY?

RAISED EYEBROWS!

SMILING MOUTH!

ROSY CHEEKS!

SPARKLING EYES!

WHY DO WE FEEL HAPPY?

FEELING HAPPY IS AN IMPORTANT EMOTION.

Human beings live together in a society. Everyone has a part to play.

We all want to do different things.

WHEN I GROW UP...
DOCTOR
SCIENTIST
ASTRONAUT

SING! EXPLORE!

When we feel happy, we feel good.

THINGS THAT MAKE US HAPPY

LOVED ONES!

MUSIC!

FAVOURITE THINGS!

14

WHEN FEELING HAPPY IS GOOD

Feeling happy is a great feeling. It can help us to know when things we are doing, or people in our lives, are good for us.

When we are happy, others around us will feel happy too. This can mean we make lots of new friends, and help others.

WHEN FEELING HAPPY IS BAD

Feeling happy doesn't always tell us something is good for us…

Too much of a good thing can be **unhealthy**.

…some things can make us feel good, but are actually bad for us.

Feeling happy is great. But you should always listen to your other emotions too. Pretending to be happy when you are not is a bad idea.

DEALING WITH FEELINGS

Captain Cheerful can share her happiness. Agents of F.E.E.L.S: GO!

LET'S HELP!

THE END 23

GLOSSARY

ACHIEVE	get something by trying hard
BODY LANGUAGE	things a person does with their body that tell you how they feel
EMOTIONS	a strong feeling such as joy, hatred, sorrow, or fear
INFECTIOUS	easily spread around
REACT	act or respond to something that has happened or been done
RELAXED	calm and not tense
ROSY	deep pink in colour
SOCIETY	a collection of people living together in a group
UNHEALTHY	harmful to your health

INDEX